RO‾

_____

1

_____

This book ⌐

The loan m
a further pe

The NASTY paSt

By
John Wood

Disease

BookLife
PUBLISHING

©2019
BookLife Publishing Ltd.
King's Lynn
Norfolk PE30 4LS

All rights reserved.
Printed in Malaysia.

A catalogue record for this book is
available from the British Library.

ISBN: 978-1-78637-591-9

Written by:
John Wood

Edited by:
Madeline Tyler

Designed by:
Dan Scase

All facts, statistics, web addresses
and URLs in this book were verified
as valid and accurate at time of
writing. No responsibility for any
changes to external websites or
references can be accepted by
either the author or publisher.

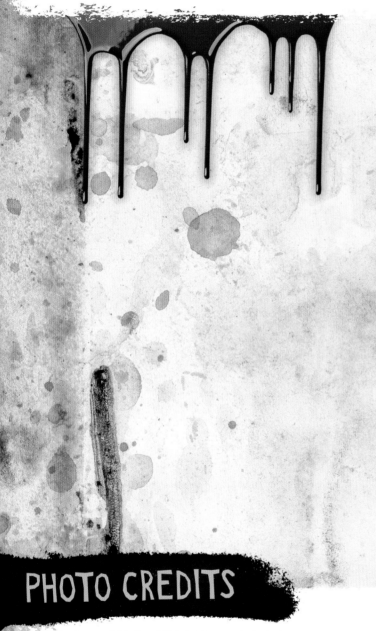

Contents

Words that look like **THIS** are explained in the glossary on page 31.

A Discovery from the Past

SOMEWHERE, DEEP IN A MUSEUM...

There are secrets underground. It's not all dirt and mud, especially if you know where to look. Buried under all that earth and rock are clues to the past. Whether it's bones, bodies, books or weapons, each clue tells a story of something that happened a long time ago. And it turns out that these stories can be pretty gruesome...

The people who find and study old, historical objects are called archaeologists (say: ar-kee-ol-uh-jists).

The past wasn't a friendly place. People didn't live as long as they do now, and there were plenty of things to kill them before they even reached old age. Towns were dirty, work was brutal, and disease and war were everywhere. Despite all this, people still made pottery and jewellery, built homes and temples, and lived their lives. Some of the things they made are still in the earth with their bones, waiting to be found...

It might not seem like it, but these archaeologists are very, very excited right now.

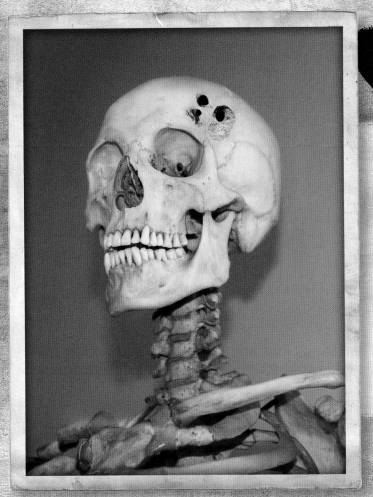

Here in this museum, all sorts of objects are collected so people can learn about history. There are even old skeletons of people who died long ago. Look, here is one! The bones look very old and worn. This person must have lived hundreds, maybe thousands of years ago. This was found in China. Look at the head – are those holes? Yes – there are three holes in the skull. What happened to this person all that time ago? Who were they, and how did they die?

The **REMAINS** show that they could have had some kind of disease. But to find out exactly how this person met their end, you must travel through history. Take a note of each disease you learn about and see if any of them might explain our skeleton here. But be careful – the past can be very, very dangerous.

Bubonic Plague

RATS, FLEAS AND LICE

In medieval times (A.D. 400s to 1400s), towns and cities were much dirtier than they are now. People didn't wash themselves much, which meant that everyone smelled really, really bad. However, that wasn't the worst thing about a world with hardly any baths. It also meant that people were often covered with fleas and lice. Fleas and lice spread disease, including the bubonic **PLAGUE**. Some historians believe that rats helped spread the plague by carrying fleas. Cities were full of rats, so you can guess what happened next...

Fleas would pass on the plague to humans by biting them.

EVERYBODY GOT THE PLAGUE

The bubonic plague was a really disgusting disease. First, people would feel ill, as if they had the flu. Then buboes would start to grow – these are swollen bumps on the skin, usually found in the armpits, on the neck or near the **GROIN**. They were black and painful, and sometimes they even burst! As horrible as bursting buboes are, people were less likely to survive if the buboes didn't burst.

During the 14th **CENTURY**, people did not like doctors. This was because doctors were too scared to treat people with the plague in case they caught it. They also looked much scarier!

THE BLACK DEATH

Long ago in history, there weren't always hospitals or doctors that people could go to, especially if they were poor. Because of this, the plague was very deadly. One of the worst **OUTBREAKS** of the bubonic plague in history was called the Black Death. Historians think that it started in China around 1334, and then spread across the world in the 1300s. This disease travelled very quickly. When it got to Europe, it **INFECTED** a huge number of people. Entire towns were completely wiped out, and between 30-60% of the **POPULATION** was killed. Sometimes there weren't enough people left to bury the dead!

The Black Death killed tens of millions of people.

It would take around three to five days for people to become sick after getting bitten by fleas or lice. After another three to five days, the person might get better. However, it was more likely that they would be dead by then.

Nobody knew what caused the plague at the time. That didn't stop them from guessing, though. Some people thought it was a punishment from God, while others thought it was to do with the planets. Some doctors even thought it was caused by wearing pointed shoes! Medicine has come a long way since medieval times...

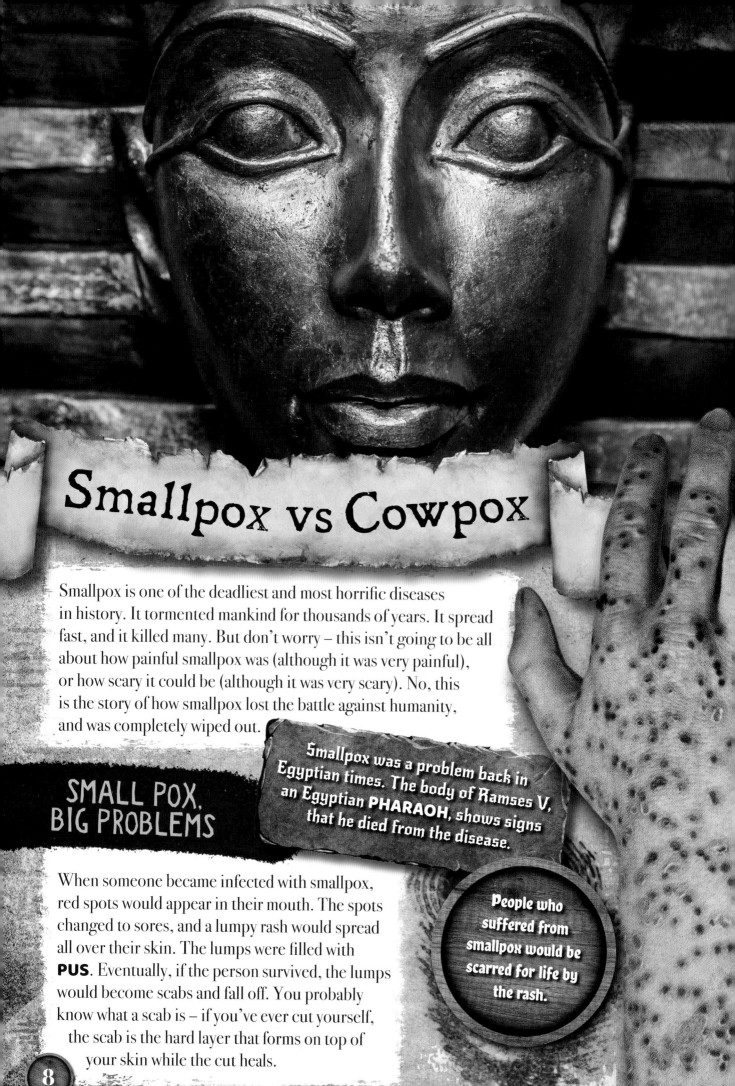

Smallpox vs Cowpox

Smallpox is one of the deadliest and most horrific diseases in history. It tormented mankind for thousands of years. It spread fast, and it killed many. But don't worry – this isn't going to be all about how painful smallpox was (although it was very painful), or how scary it could be (although it was very scary). No, this is the story of how smallpox lost the battle against humanity, and was completely wiped out.

SMALL POX, BIG PROBLEMS

Smallpox was a problem back in Egyptian times. The body of Ramses V, an Egyptian **PHARAOH**, shows signs that he died from the disease.

People who suffered from smallpox would be scarred for life by the rash.

When someone became infected with smallpox, red spots would appear in their mouth. The spots changed to sores, and a lumpy rash would spread all over their skin. The lumps were filled with **PUS**. Eventually, if the person survived, the lumps would become scabs and fall off. You probably know what a scab is – if you've ever cut yourself, the scab is the hard layer that forms on top of your skin while the cut heals.

FINDING THE CURE

Things really began to change in 1796. A man called Edward Jenner had heard stories that milkmaids and farmers who got a disease called cowpox didn't ever catch smallpox. To see if this was true, Jenner grabbed an unlucky eight-year-old boy called James Phipps and scratched him with a needle full of cowpox. The cowpox made James ill, but he soon got better. Then Jenner scratched him with another needle – this time full of the deadly smallpox!

Cowpox looked a lot like smallpox, but it was much less likely to kill anyone.

AN UNEXPECTED TURN

However, something amazing happened. James didn't get ill from the smallpox. It turns out that cowpox acts as a vaccine (say: vak-seen) – this means it teaches the body how to fight other diseases that are similar. Cowpox and smallpox are similar, and James's body easily fought off the deadly disease. However, it was almost 200 years before smallpox finally disappeared. Each time there was an outbreak, people in the area were given vaccines. The last reported case of the disease was in 1977.

This painting shows Edward Jenner scratching cowpox into James Phipps' arm. Ouch!

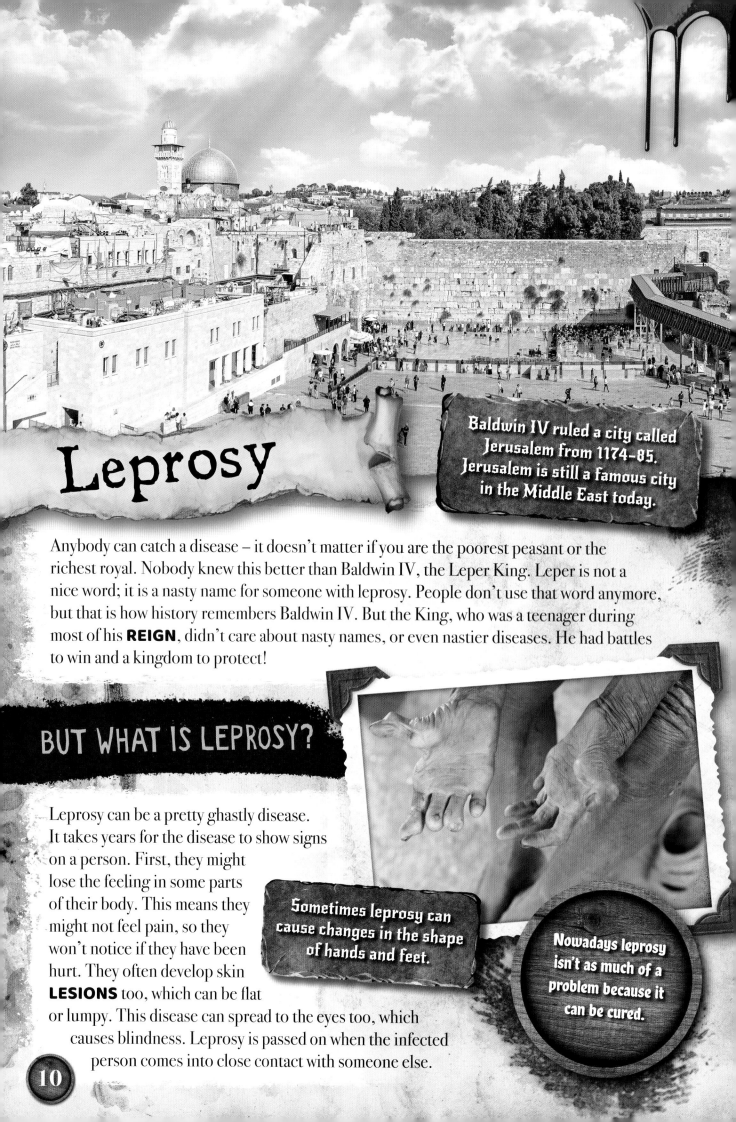

Leprosy

Baldwin IV ruled a city called Jerusalem from 1174–85. Jerusalem is still a famous city in the Middle East today.

Anybody can catch a disease – it doesn't matter if you are the poorest peasant or the richest royal. Nobody knew this better than Baldwin IV, the Leper King. Leper is not a nice word; it is a nasty name for someone with leprosy. People don't use that word anymore, but that is how history remembers Baldwin IV. But the King, who was a teenager during most of his **REIGN**, didn't care about nasty names, or even nastier diseases. He had battles to win and a kingdom to protect!

BUT WHAT IS LEPROSY?

Leprosy can be a pretty ghastly disease. It takes years for the disease to show signs on a person. First, they might lose the feeling in some parts of their body. This means they might not feel pain, so they won't notice if they have been hurt. They often develop skin **LESIONS** too, which can be flat or lumpy. This disease can spread to the eyes too, which causes blindness. Leprosy is passed on when the infected person comes into close contact with someone else.

Sometimes leprosy can cause changes in the shape of hands and feet.

Nowadays leprosy isn't as much of a problem because it can be cured.

FEAR AND LEPROSY

The lesions caused by leprosy could make people look strange. This made others scared, so people with the disease were often sent away to live apart from everyone else.

In some areas of the world, people with leprosy had to wear signs and ring bells to warn people that they were coming.

THE LEPER KING

However, Baldwin IV had no intention of going away from his people, and they didn't want him to go either. When he became king at the age of 13, his tutor already knew Baldwin had leprosy because the young king couldn't feel anything in most of his right arm. The people loved the King; he was good at horse riding, and he was brave and intelligent. As he got older, the disease worsened. Soon he was covered in lesions and ulcers, but his people stayed loyal, and he still fought on the battlefield to protect Jerusalem. At the age of 16, even though he could only use one hand and needed help putting his armour on, Baldwin won a huge battle against a much bigger army led by a man called Saladin. Baldwin continued to be a brave and clever king until he died.

At the end of his life, Baldwin IV went blind and had to be carried around in a LITTER.

Plague of Athens

Historians think that they are really clever. They'll go on for hours about how long the Roman Empire lasted, or when the first aeroplane was invented. However, if you really want to shut them up, ask them about the plague of Athens. If they say they know exactly what happened, then they are telling lies!

It's no good looking in your books, Mr Historian! You won't find the answer there!

NOBODY KNOWS WHAT THE PLAGUE OF ATHENS WAS

Between 430 and 427 B.C., there was a terrible disease in Athens, the capital city of **ANCIENT** Greece. It is thought to have killed around 300,000 people, and it lasted for four years. Some historians even think it was one of the reasons that the powerful ancient Greek **CIVILISATION** was destroyed. But nobody knows exactly what the disease was, even to this day. There is a reason for this – there isn't much information about it. In fact, only one man wrote about it, and he was called Thucydides (say: thoo-sid-ih-deez).

Luckily, Thucydides knew a lot about the disease – he caught it!

It is thought that one in three people died in Athens during the plague.

TAKE IT AWAY, THUCYDIDES

Here are some of the **SYMPTOMS** that Thucydides described:

- Violent heats in the head
- Redness of the eyes
- Terrible breath
- Vomiting
- Ulcers and patches of skin full of pus
- Throat and tongue covered with blood

People's skin also went very red, and they would cough and sneeze a lot. They would get so hot that they couldn't stand to have any clothes on, and some people jumped in cold water to cool down. Many were dead in nine days.

THE PELOPONNESIAN WAR

At the time, Thucydides was meant to be writing about the Peloponnesian War, which started in 431 B.C. This was a war between the Athenians and the Spartans. The Spartans were some of the best fighters in the world, especially on land. During the war, the Athenians lost a lot of their ships, and had to defend the city of Athens from the Spartans. This was a difficult task, but the plague made everything much worse. It is thought that the plague killed up to a quarter of their army. The Athenians lost the war, and their great civilisation never recovered.

Typhoid Fever

THE SYMPTOMS

If you had typhoid fever, you would probably have a headache. You would probably cough, ache, and have a body temperature of up to 40 degrees Celsius (°C). Then, if you lived a long time ago, you would probably die. Although this sounds terrible, there are some people who don't feel ill at all when they get typhoid fever. But it turns out that this can be even worse for everyone...

Typhoid fever also makes it difficult to poo, or causes runny poo.

A STORY ABOUT TYPHOID FEVER

In the old days, you could never be sure who's sneezed in your stew...

In New York, 1907, a man called Mr Warren took his family on holiday to a summer house. However, while staying there, his wife, daughters and maids all became ill with typhoid fever. Mr Warren couldn't work out what was making everyone ill. But then he hired a man called Mr Soper to investigate. Mr Soper worked out that it came from the family's cook, Mary Mallon. He found out that 22 people had caught typhoid fever in the places Mary had worked before. She was a healthy carrier of the disease – this means that she did not feel the effects of typhoid, but she passed it on to other people.

However, to be absolutely sure that Mary had typhoid fever, Mr Soper would need to do tests. So the next day, he marched into Mary's place of work and asked her for samples of her blood, poo and wee. Then Mary chased him out of the building with a carving fork. Mr Soper thought long and hard about what to do, and decided to let the New York City Health Department deal with Mary. Mary was caught and sent to a cottage in New York which was separate from everyone else.

The cottage in New York was here, on North Brother Island.

Mary became quite famous, and was nicknamed Typhoid Mary. She has become a famous example of how important it is to quarantine people with **CONTAGIOUS** diseases. When someone is quarantined, they are taken away from healthy people until they are cured. Unfortunately for Mary, this meant that she couldn't cook for anyone. It turns out you don't even have to get ill from a disease for it to ruin your life.

Being quarantined is only important if the disease is deadly and easily spread.

Scurvy

STRUGGLES AT SEA

There is only one thing scarier than a pirate, and that is a pirate with bleeding gums and awful, awful breath. Unfortunately, this is exactly the kind of pirate you might have come across if you lived any time from the 1400s to the 1700s. This is because many pirates had a disease called scurvy. In fact, if you sailed across the oceans during this period of history, many sailors would have looked just as ill – scurvy was a real problem for those at sea.

THE IMPORTANCE OF FRUIT

More than two million sailors died from scurvy from the 15th to the mid-19th century.

Scurvy is a disease that occurs in people who don't eat enough foods that contain vitamin C. Vitamin C mainly comes from fruits and vegetables, especially citrus fruits such as oranges and lemons. However, if you didn't get any vitamin C for over three months, you might start to get scurvy. There are still some people today who develop this disease. However, it was a much bigger problem for people sailing the seas long ago. This is because there weren't many fresh fruits and vegetables on the ships – they were stocked with grains, and other foods that would last a long time.

Pirates like this had seen all the high seas, but never the vitamin Cs.

PAST THE GUMS

Not only did the gums begin to bleed and **SWELL**, but the skin would turn black and their faces became shrunken. This was because the flesh was dying. Teeth fell out, and those affected would find it difficult to move and breathe. Scurvy could change a person's personality too – they might act like someone different. They might not taste, smell or hear very well either. The only chance of recovery was if the sailors and pirates could get some vitamin C.

A lack of vitamin C causes the body to break down.

Many trips around the oceans were marked by scurvy. When a famous explorer called Magellan tried to sail around the world, he lost around half of his crew because of this disease. Many historians say that scurvy took more sailors' lives than storms, shipwrecks, fighting and other diseases put together. In the end, it doesn't matter if you are a fearsome pirate, a brave explorer or a child at school – everyone needs to eat their fruit and vegetables.

Although some people realised that citrus fruits seemed to help with scurvy, the cure wasn't well known until centuries later.

Lead Poisoning

For most of history, people have agreed on one thing: lead (say: led) was great. Lead is a type of metal. It is good at many things – it can be used to make plumbing, makeup, coins, cups, paint, plates, pots and pans. It is useful, it is everywhere and it is cheap. Unfortunately, it is also very, very poisonous.

These coins are made from lead.

LEAD IN THE BELLY

When lead gets into the body, it causes lead poisoning. Long ago, not everyone knew how serious this disease was. People in history got lead poisoning in all sorts of ways; lead could seep into the skin if it was used in makeup, or it would get into the stomach if it was used as food **SEASONING**. If someone drank water from a lead mug, the lead could seep into the water, and then get into the body.

Egyptian eye makeup contained lead.

FALL OF ROME

People with lead poisoning might feel pain in their stomach, muscles or head. It caused people's skin to look wrinkly and old. But worst of all was the effect on their brains – this disease would cause people to lose their minds. First, they would become gloomy and miserable. Eventually they would always feel tired and would forget things all the time.

This Roman plumbing was uncovered in modern-day Georgia.

The Romans actually did know lead was bad for their health, but they kept on using it anyway. They thought that, as long as they didn't spend all day in the lead mines, they wouldn't be too badly affected, so they sent the **SLAVES** down the mines instead. But they were wrong. Roman plumbing – all the pipes that brought them water – was made of lead, so even the rich Romans who weren't mining were still swallowing lead all day. Many historians think that lead poisoning explains a lot of the odd behaviour of Roman emperors, and that this disease was one of the things that destroyed the whole Roman Empire.

Bloodletting

If you went to a doctor with a fever in ancient Roman or Greek times, you wouldn't get a handful of pills, or a note for a week off school and a good rest, either. The doctor would be more likely to say you had too much blood in your body! He might also say there was only one way to fix it – let some out!

No doctor! You don't have to drain my blood! I feel much better – honest!

This type of treatment was called bloodletting. It was done in almost every part of the ancient world, from ancient Egypt to China, as well as ancient Rome to ancient Greece. Nowadays, there are some types of illness that might mean the doctor has to let some blood out of the patient. However, this is not very common. In the olden days, bloodletting was used to try and cure all sorts of things, from headaches to **VERTIGO**. However, that doesn't mean it worked...

BLOODLETTING DIDN'T SAVE THE PRESIDENT

George Washington was the first president of the United States of America. He was president from 1789 to 1797. In 1799, Washington was struck down by a mysterious disease. The doctors took away almost half of all the blood in his body to cure him. George Washington died later that night.

GEORGE WASHINGTON

THE FOUR HUMOURS

Ancient Greek doctors and **PHILOSOPHERS** (say: fill-oss-o-fers) such as Hippocrates (say: hip-ok-ra-tees) and Thucydides realised that diseases and illnesses had nothing to do with prayers and gods. They were caused by problems in the body. They came up with the idea of the four humours, which was the idea that the body has four fluids inside, and there needed to be an even amount of each one. The four humours were phlegm (snot), yellow bile (vomit), black bile (more vomit) and blood. If the doctors thought that the four humours were out of balance, they might get rid of some blood to even it out. That is one of the reasons that bloodletting was so popular.

Although Hippocrates and his friends were very, very smart, this idea was very, very wrong. Not your best work, Hippocrates.

BRING ON THE LEECHES

Throughout history, there have been many ways that blood has been let out of the body. Often, doctors simply cut the skin with a knife. However, it was hard to stop the bleeding when it was started this way. Leeches were a popular way of letting blood out of the body. Leeches are tiny creatures that bite other animals and suck the blood out.

LEECH

The Dancing Plague

A STORY MOST STRANGE...

One day, in 1518, a woman started dancing. There was no music or reason to dance, but that didn't matter to her. Her name was Frau Troffea, and she lived in a city called Strasbourg, in what is now France. On that first day, people laughed and cheered. However, when Frau Troffea hadn't stopped on the second day, the laughing and cheering stopped. By the sixth day, as Frau Troffea continued to dance without a single break, 34 people joined her in her dancing. Suddenly, the city of Strasbourg realised they were dealing with a very, very strange disease.

Nobody knew what to do. At first they thought the dancers' blood had become too hot. To try and cure them, the town set up a stage, and invited musicians to play. However, this was a terrible idea – more and more people joined the non-stop dancing. People danced until they were too tired to stand up. Their feet were bloody, and many died from heart attacks and **EXHAUSTION**.

It is thought that 400 people were part of this dance **TRANCE**.

MUSICIANS

One writer who lived nearby said that 15 people were dying every day during the worst part of the dancing plague.

Two months after the dancing plague started, it stopped. There didn't seem to be any reason for this. Historians have tried to work out what caused it – some think that it was caused by eating something that caused **HALLUCINATIONS**, while others think that they danced for religious reasons. However, most historians believe that the dancing was connected to an illness of the mind – it was probably caused by stress and unhappiness.

WHAT CAUSED THE DANCING?

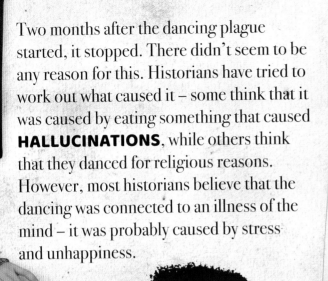

There were lots of reasons why the people of Strasbourg were unhappy; horrible diseases like smallpox were around every corner, and there were many **FAMINES** around that time. A writer in Strasbourg said that 1517 was a bad year; food was getting more expensive, and there were many **CONFLICTS** going on at the time. Luckily, this was the last time a dancing plague struck Europe.

There have been no reports of anything like this happening in today's world... yet.

Yellow Fever

This is a mosquito. They are small, buzzing insects that bite humans and suck a small amount of blood. Although they might not look dangerous, mosquitos have been infecting humans with many deadly diseases for thousands of years. One of these diseases is called yellow fever. Unfortunately, for a long time, humans didn't realise that these tiny things were behind such a terrible illness.

WHAT IS YELLOW FEVER?

Some people who caught yellow fever would only get normal flu symptoms – they would vomit, not want to eat and have headaches and backaches. However, other people would enter a second stage of the disease which was much worse. Along with the flu symptoms already mentioned, their skin would turn yellow, their wee would be dark and their vomit would be black. They would have pains in their body, and might even bleed from their mouths, noses, eyes or stomachs.

Half of the patients who entered the second stage of yellow fever would die in less than ten days.

SPAIN

A HISTORY OF YELLOW FEVER

It is thought that the disease started in Africa, in monkeys. Eventually the disease found its way to humans, thanks to the mosquitos. When sailing **TECHNOLOGY** got better, there were a lot more boats travelling between Africa, America and Europe. The mosquitos came with the boats, and the disease spread all over the world. In the 1600s, there were lots of outbreaks of yellow fever in America. In 1730, there was an outbreak all over Europe, with 2,200 deaths reported in Spain alone.

Silly doctors! It was mosquitos all along!

Yellow fever has probably been around for at least 3,000 years.

Up until the 19th century, doctors still thought the disease was spread by human-to-human contact. But they were all wrong. Luckily, a Cuban clever-clogs called Carlos Finlay showed up and, in 1881, proved that it was spread by mosquitos all along. However, nobody listened to him, and it wasn't until 1900 that people started to deal with mosquitos to fight yellow fever.

Tuberculosis

Tuberculosis, also called TB, has been around for a long time. We're not sure exactly when it first showed up – some **SCIENTISTS** think TB was killing humans 70,000 years ago, while others think that it started around 6,000 years ago. Either way, TB has been a problem for humans since before written history began. Over time, TB has been called many things. Here are just a few names used to describe it.

PHTHISIS

TB has also been found in the spines of ancient Egyptian mummies. Poor mummies.

In ancient Greece, Hippocrates wrote about a disease that caused lots of coughing and wheezing. People with the disease would become thin and tired, and might have a fever. He called it phthisis (say: f-thy-siss), but he was actually writing about TB. TB usually develops slowly in the **LUNGS**, which affects a person's breathing. TB could be spread through the air when people coughed or spoke, and it affected everyone, young and old.

Sometimes people would even cough up blood!

KING'S EVIL

In the Middle Ages, a skin illness called scrofula, caused by TB, was known as 'The King's Evil'. Although it was not written about much, archaeologists have found lots of **EVIDENCE** that TB existed all over Europe. During this time, people believed that if a king or queen touched them, they would get better. This was called 'the royal touch'. Hundreds and thousands of people queued up to see kings and queens in order to be cured. The king or queen would lay their hands on the person with scrofula, and then they would say a prayer. Unfortunately, there is no evidence that this did them any good at all.

In the 18th century, TB was called the white plague, because of how pale people became when they were infected.

CONSUMPTION

During the 19th century, TB was often called consumption. Consumption was a name for any disease that caused people to get thin and weak, although TB was often the real cause. It killed many people, including lots of artists and famous people. TB also had another name during this time which was much scarier: 'Captain among These Men of Death.'

One in four deaths were caused by TB for much of the 19th century.

Trephining

Surgery today is very complicated stuff. There are lots of strange-looking tools and important-looking doctors who have spent years and years studying medicine. But how far back do you think surgery goes? Any good historian will tell you that surgery has been around, although in many different forms, for thousands and thousands of years. On this page, we are going to learn about one of the oldest types of surgery: trephining.

Surgery can be a way of curing all sorts of diseases.

These holes were no accident.

WHAT IS TREPHINING?

Trephining is when a hole is drilled into somebody's head using certain tools. Archaeologists have found more and more ancient skulls with these holes. This might not seem strange, but when archaeologists look closely, they can often see that the bone around these holes has healed slightly. This tells them that people survived these holes for a long time after they were done.

WHERE AND WHEN?

THE STONE AGE ENDED OVER 4,000 YEARS AGO.

People have been trephining as far back as the Stone Age. Trephined skulls have been found all over the world, from Peru, in South America, to China, in Asia. However, nobody is exactly sure why it was done. People have made some guesses, though.

MOST IMPORTANTLY... WHY?

Many of the skulls found had other problems, which might mean that trephining was a way of treating head injuries and getting rid of pain. However, other skulls were in perfect condition, except for the massive holes caused by trephining. This means that this surgery might have been a way of treating diseases that affected the brain in ways that couldn't be seen on the outside. People at the time might have thought that evil spirits were trapped inside, and drilling a hole would let the spirit out. Trephining might have even been part of a **RITUAL** that everyone had to go through in some groups.

This skull has eight holes, and was found in Papua New Guinea.

A650847

29

Mystery Solved?

Did you find anything that explains our skeleton, here in the museum? If you said trephining, well done! The holes in the skeleton's skull perfectly match the holes in other skulls that went through trephination. The skeleton is also very old, which would make sense because trephining has been done for thousands of years.

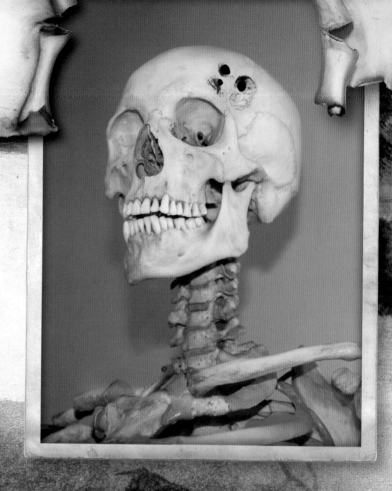

Perhaps this person was alive during the Stone Age. They might have been a hunter for their tribe. They might have had a family. Maybe one day their head hurt for no reason at all – the tribe might have been very confused and worried.

After their head didn't stop hurting, the wisest of the tribe might have said that evil spirits were the problem, and that trephining was the only answer. The holes look like they have healed – our person probably survived the surgery and felt better. Maybe they went hunting to celebrate! If it was true, this is just one of the many stories that survive through time and history and teach us about the past.

Glossary

ANCIENT belonging to the very distant past and no longer in existence

CENTURY a period of 100 years

CIVILISATION the society, culture and way of life of a certain area

CONFLICTS active disagreements between people

CONTAGIOUS (of a disease) able to spread from one person to another

EVIDENCE a trace or indication of something

EXHAUSTION the feeling of being very tired and having little energy

FAMINES times when large numbers of people do not have enough food

GROIN the area between the legs

HALLUCINATIONS seeing, hearing or feeling things that seem real, but aren't

INFECTED having caught a disease and showing symptoms

LESIONS damaged bits of skin or body tissue that are caused by injury or disease

LITTER a chair or throne in which a person is carried around

LUNGS bag-like organs that some animals use to breathe

OUTBREAKS when something suddenly happens, usually when talking about war or diseases

PHARAOH a ruler in ancient Egypt

PHILOSOPHERS people who study the nature of knowledge, reality and existence

PLAGUE a disease that spreads quickly to many people; usually talking about diseases in history

POPULATION the number of people living in a place

PUS a thick yellowish or green fluid produced by the body

REIGN the period of time that a leader rules for

REMAINS parts that have been left behind; of a building, artifact or body

RITUAL ordered action that takes place during religious ceremonies

SCIENTISTS people who study and know a lot about science

SEASONING things put in food to make it more flavourful

SLAVES people who have no freedom and are owned by another person

SWELL grow larger or expand

SYMPTOMS things that happen in the body suggesting that there is a disease or disorder

TECHNOLOGY machines or devices that are made using scientific knowledge

TRANCE a state that seems to be between being asleep and awake

VERTIGO a feeling of dizziness and a loss of balance, usually caused by disease or looking down from great heights

Index